The Jigsaw of Eight Thousand Pieces

SOUL REFLECTIONS

DIANNE CIKUSA

Copyright © Dianne Cikusa 2020

The moral right of the author has been asserted in accordance with the Copyright Amendment (Moral Rights) Act 2000.

All rights reserved. Except as permitted under the Australian Copyright Act 1968 (for example, fair dealing for the purposes of study, research, criticism or review) no part of this publication may be reproduced, stored in a retrieval system, or transmitted in any form or by any means, electronic, mechanical, photocopying, recording or otherwise, without the written permission of the publisher.

Cataloguing-in-Publication entry is available from the National Library of Australia: http://catalogue.nla.gov.au/

Title: The Jigsaw of Eight Thousand Pieces
Subtitle: Soul reflections
Author: Cikusa, Dianne, 1973–
ISBNs: 978-0-9943257-8-5 (paperback)
Subjects: BODY, MIND & SPIRIT: Inspiration & Personal Growth;
           PHILOSOPHY: Mind & Body;
           SELF-HELP: Motivational & Inspirational; Personal Growth / General

Cover and internal images under license from Adobe Stock
Cover design by Ally Mosher @ allymosher.com

Published by Mignon Press, 2020
PO Box 922, Katoomba NSW 2780

mignon PRESS

Also by Dianne Cikusa:

The Rain Sermon: Le Sermon de la Pluie

The Sea In-Between

Hope and Substance

Who saw Beauty cry, and failed to hold her left hand?

Smile...

Not because you like what you see, but because you accept who you are.

Laugh...

Not because what you see is funny, but because you are detached from the antics of the world.

Cry...

Not because you are sad, but for the preciousness of moments too hard to grasp.

2 The Jigsaw of Eight Thousand Pieces

We will only get 'out' of life the awareness that we put into it.

4 The Jigsaw of Eight Thousand Pieces

Act for the good of the Soul, not for the bliss of thy Self.

6   The Jigsaw of Eight Thousand Pieces

Simplify the equation to better understand the problem.

8 The Jigsaw of Eight Thousand Pieces

Humility takes the world at its own level of love.

The Jigsaw of Eight Thousand Pieces

When joy is bottled, love can't be poured.

The Jigsaw of Eight Thousand Pieces

Resentment hardens by losing patience.

The Jigsaw of Eight Thousand Pieces

One must finish writing the play, before consciousness can act in it.

The Jigsaw of Eight Thousand Pieces

Thoughts escort the blind;
Wisdom leads the enlightened heart.

The Jigsaw of Eight Thousand Pieces

Life moves smoothly within the self of appreciation.

The Jigsaw of Eight Thousand Pieces

Fight first personal integrity, before you defend against world injustice.

The Jigsaw of Eight Thousand Pieces

'Taking more' duly obliges us to give more purposeful use of that energy.

The Jigsaw of Eight Thousand Pieces

A long life of compassion...
can commence in a single
day.

The Jigsaw of Eight Thousand Pieces

Fear has love to get;
Faith has loving work to go
on with.

The Jigsaw of Eight Thousand Pieces

Nothing... is actually not nothing.

30 The Jigsaw of Eight Thousand Pieces

Our spirit is always bigger, and better equipped for love.

The Jigsaw of Eight Thousand Pieces

A sole experience is nonetheless capable of changing the world, when applied with delicate and observant precision.

The Jigsaw of Eight Thousand Pieces

Read about enlightenment [...then assess afterwards your veritable comprehension].

The Jigsaw of Eight Thousand Pieces

There are as many guiding pilots, as there are flight paths and nominated schedules.

The Jigsaw of Eight Thousand Pieces

Flow is constantly attentive.

The Jigsaw of Eight Thousand Pieces

The best impact absorbs most lightly.

The Jigsaw of Eight Thousand Pieces

Love grows by tireless respect.

The Jigsaw of Eight Thousand Pieces

Seek out depth first, then explore its psychic surroundings.

The Jigsaw of Eight Thousand Pieces

Read behind the page;
look beneath the mask.

The Jigsaw of Eight Thousand Pieces

Wars cannot end, if hatred won't sit still.

The Jigsaw of Eight Thousand Pieces

Higher energy knows 'when' to find you, and 'where' to subconsciously send you.

The Jigsaw of Eight Thousand Pieces

Creativity unblocks in stages.

The Jigsaw of Eight Thousand Pieces

Products have depreciating value, where they have collected manufactured importance.

The Jigsaw of Eight Thousand Pieces

It will all make sense later... Catch up to later.

The Jigsaw of Eight Thousand Pieces

God will keep pulling your leg… until you aren't afraid to laugh.

The Jigsaw of Eight Thousand Pieces

Fear distinguishes a problem, whereas the Higher Mind notes a resolvable issue.

The Jigsaw of Eight Thousand Pieces

Say 'I love you', then go back and prove it.

The Jigsaw of Eight Thousand Pieces

Sponge the earthly certainty from your body (so that you won't feel so hard to die).

The Jigsaw of Eight Thousand Pieces

A wise teacher provides just enough challenge.

The Jigsaw of Eight Thousand Pieces

Money only pretends to make a man supreme, and a woman more beautiful.

The Jigsaw of Eight Thousand Pieces

Where an 'energy' will not move in our current favour, it requires that we draw rather from its essence.

The Jigsaw of Eight Thousand Pieces

Only the Spirit retains an invincible sense of humour.

The Jigsaw of Eight Thousand Pieces

Turn over both guilty parties to the balancing judge.

The Jigsaw of Eight Thousand Pieces

Phone me in heaven; your death lives there too.

The Jigsaw of Eight Thousand Pieces

Love both your parents, since it took two to make the baby.

The Jigsaw of Eight Thousand Pieces

Higher discernment consumes the same world, but with far less attachment.

The Jigsaw of Eight Thousand Pieces

Surrender is akin to the following of one's interior design.

The Jigsaw of Eight Thousand Pieces

Enough 'compassion' won't react to a slighting provocation.

The Jigsaw of Eight Thousand Pieces

Hope is simply unrefined faith.

The Jigsaw of Eight Thousand Pieces

Real love takes no lesson away.

The Jigsaw of Eight Thousand Pieces

The best defence -- is ready for a simple moment.

The Jigsaw of Eight Thousand Pieces

Joy has no more or less problems.

The Jigsaw of Eight Thousand Pieces

Copy God, until you resemble the uncomplicated original.

The Jigsaw of Eight Thousand Pieces

Compassion says less [and means more].

The Jigsaw of Eight Thousand Pieces

Forgiveness was a doormat
[-- that said 'thankyou'].

The Jigsaw of Eight Thousand Pieces

Incarnate again into the world... with least blinded eyes.

The Jigsaw of Eight Thousand Pieces

If your own life agrees with you, no other opinion needs to.

The Jigsaw of Eight Thousand Pieces

Tune emptiness, so that death unfolds naturally.

The Jigsaw of Eight Thousand Pieces

If you're bored, challenge your guilt.

The Jigsaw of Eight Thousand Pieces

An awakened soul sees everything with lucid spontaneity.

The Jigsaw of Eight Thousand Pieces

Self-worth -- has been aimed a worthy bullet.

The Jigsaw of Eight Thousand Pieces

How creatively can you say,
'I don't want to die'?

The Jigsaw of Eight Thousand Pieces

An extremely loving God goes out of His way to put you back on track.

The Jigsaw of Eight Thousand Pieces

See the larger world
as each small life is
feeling it.

The Jigsaw of Eight Thousand Pieces

Choose emotional freedom,
or an easy cage.

The Jigsaw of Eight Thousand Pieces

While Soul remembers the way, ego creates the traffic conditions.

The Jigsaw of Eight Thousand Pieces

Mind your ignorance;
mind your knowledge.

The Jigsaw of Eight Thousand Pieces

You didn't change the face of ugly from inside.

The Jigsaw of Eight Thousand Pieces

Don't ruin a perfectly good moment. Say nothing.

The Jigsaw of Eight Thousand Pieces

Wisdom knows precisely what <u>not</u> to do.

The Jigsaw of Eight Thousand Pieces

In the moment of grief, only love mattered.

The Jigsaw of Eight Thousand Pieces

Once you know the emotional moves, you can dance with any-body.

The Jigsaw of Eight Thousand Pieces

It is a kindred heart that imparts to us the gift of a resounding friendship.

The Jigsaw of Eight Thousand Pieces

The World is Not Going to End *If*... we find the means for restoring Love.

The Jigsaw of Eight Thousand Pieces

Stuff yourself stupid... then fill yourself smart.

The Jigsaw of Eight Thousand Pieces

So what's a few lifetimes in the land of eternity?

The Jigsaw of Eight Thousand Pieces

Leave alone those people who are still running the coarser part of their lives away.

The Jigsaw of Eight Thousand Pieces

A 'full' life equally embraces both fear and death.

The Jigsaw of Eight Thousand Pieces

All spirit gods -- are but
one ancient love.

The Jigsaw of Eight Thousand Pieces

Awareness arrives by infinite creative effort.

The Jigsaw of Eight Thousand Pieces

Joyfulness -- provides all the love you need.

The Jigsaw of Eight Thousand Pieces

You were always making perfect sense to God, even if it wasn't entirely poised before the unsympathetic eyes of The World.

The Jigsaw of Eight Thousand Pieces

'No' includes the astuteness of applying 'yes'.

The Jigsaw of Eight Thousand Pieces

When you *are* the world, you can merge seamlessly with everything else in it.

The Jigsaw of Eight Thousand Pieces

Long-lasting friends are those empowered by your memory.

The Jigsaw of Eight Thousand Pieces

Retrace the desiring mind...
for every lost truth and
losing hope.

The Jigsaw of Eight Thousand Pieces

Inner abundance grows by means of exceptional simplicity.

The Jigsaw of Eight Thousand Pieces

If the body is inwardly feeling pain, show it liberally where to breathe.

The Jigsaw of Eight Thousand Pieces

Peace is [exactly] equivalent to an acceptance of one's death.

The Jigsaw of Eight Thousand Pieces

Essence is not what is depressed -- action is.

The Jigsaw of Eight Thousand Pieces

The master is the person to whom you sold your original power.

The Jigsaw of Eight Thousand Pieces

Don't get on the impending ride, if you think you're going to be sick!

The Jigsaw of Eight Thousand Pieces

In truth, it IS a deadly game. We only forgot why we each started to play.

The Jigsaw of Eight Thousand Pieces

Karma is a serious business;

                              Life is not.

The Jigsaw of Eight Thousand Pieces

Oscillating souls -- know to work both sides of the spiritual clock.

The Jigsaw of Eight Thousand Pieces

Children make the world look innocent.

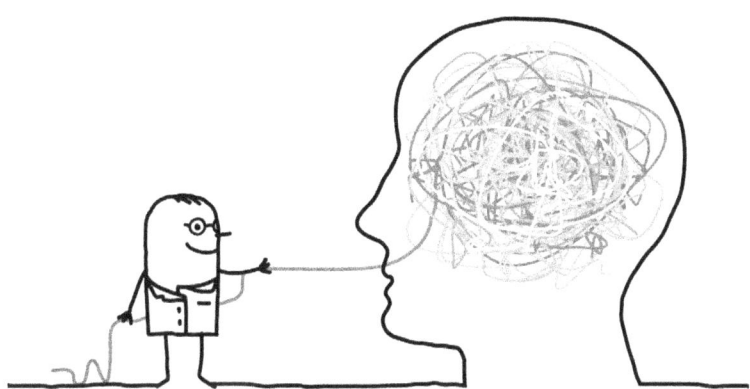

About the author

Dianne Cikusa was born in Australia in 1973. She has a Bachelor of Commerce in Marketing as well as postgraduate qualifications in foreign language studies, including linguistics and translation.

Dianne has published work in numerous online poetry journals, anthologies and writers' magazines, with an additional focus on producing digital media and merchandise. She is the author of three poetry books, including a bilingual collection. She is further engaged in the editing and production of a series of original wisdom quotes books aimed at facilitating self-awareness and personal development using a thematic approach.

The insights-quotes series encourages a 'contemporary' understanding of wisdom and its application to our everyday life via a down-to-earth approach that is relevant, attainable and functional. In a hectic world, there is less and less time to make sense of the constant influx of information with which we are bombarded so as to be able to keep 'peace' with the process of realising our own life goals. It is during these moments that we may need a simplified perspective, or a motivational 'push', in order to grasp a concept which enables us to form a clearer personal picture than before – one that is less clouded by emotional complexity or psychological factors. In so doing, we can reduce the maze of our confusion to its 'essence' and proceed with the journey and greater vision.

The writing of the author is the product of several years of acquired knowledge, training and personal discipline in diverse fields of metaphysics, theosophy, philosophy, alternative medicines and nutrition, and other forms of wholistic healing which harmonise the vital mind-body-soul relationship.

For information and links, please visit:

www.mignonpress.com

www.ingramcontent.com/pod-product-compliance
Lightning Source LLC
Chambersburg PA
CBHW080848020526
44118CB00037B/2310